Jewish Slang

coloring book

By Anna Nadler & Steven Sheffron

Copyright © 2019 Anna Nadler
All rights reserved
Published by Little Birdie Press™
No part of this publication may be
reproduced, stored in a retrieval system or
transmitted in any form or by any means,
electronic, mechanical, photocopying, recording
or otherwise, without prior written permission
from the author/publisher.
www.annanadler.com

ME-SHUG-GENEH

meshuggeneh - a person who is not making any sense, a crazy person

NOSH

nosh -
snack, light meal
to nosh, to munch
on something.

© Anna Nadler 2019
© Anna Nadler 2019
© Anna Nadler 2019
© Anna Nadler 2019
© Anna Nadler 2019
© Anna Nadler 2019
© Anna Nadler 2019

"Sometimes this child can be such a **nudnick!**"

nudnick - an extremely annoying person

Bupkes

bupkes - nothing, nada, also means, literally, goat droppings

YENTA

yenta - a woman who is a gossiper, a busybody.

© Anna Nadler 2019
© Anna Nadler 2019
© Anna Nadler 2019
© Anna Nadler 2019
© Anna Nadler 2019
© Anna Nadler 2019
© Anna Nadler 2019

Mazel Tov!

mazel tov - congratulations!

oy gevalt - a phrase used to show suprise.

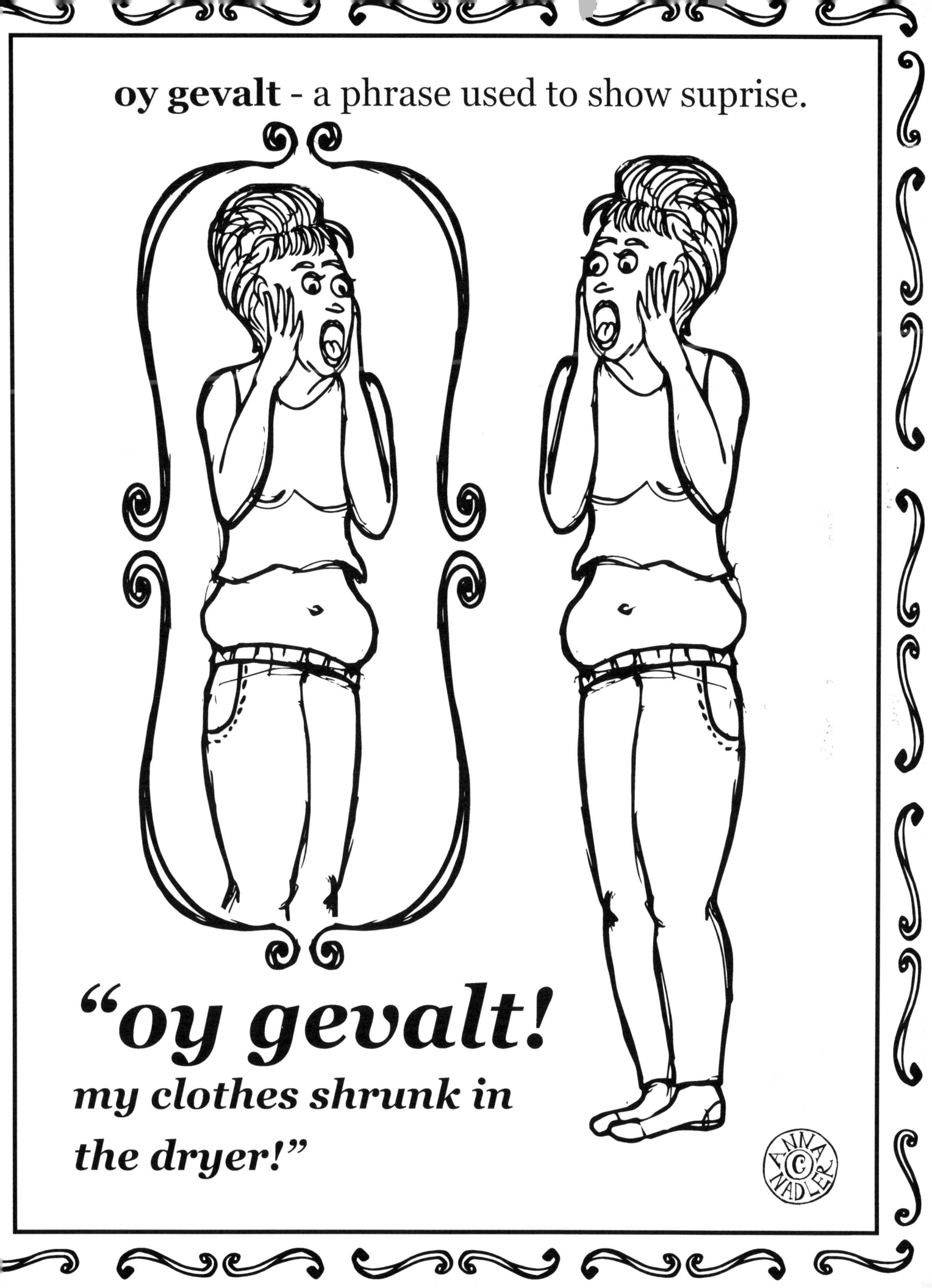

"oy gevalt!
my clothes shrunk in the dryer!"

© Anna Nadler 2019
© Anna Nadler 2019
© Anna Nadler 2019
© Anna Nadler 2019
© Anna Nadler 2019
© Anna Nadler 2019
© Anna Nadler 2019

KLUTZ

klutz - a person who is clumsy.

soul mate meant to be

true love

we fit

the one

bashert

bashert - divinely destined spouse or soul mate, one who perfectly completes the other.

© Anna Nadler 2019
© Anna Nadler 2019
© Anna Nadler 2019
© Anna Nadler 2019
© Anna Nadler 2019
© Anna Nadler 2019
© Anna Nadler 2019

FA-KAK-TA

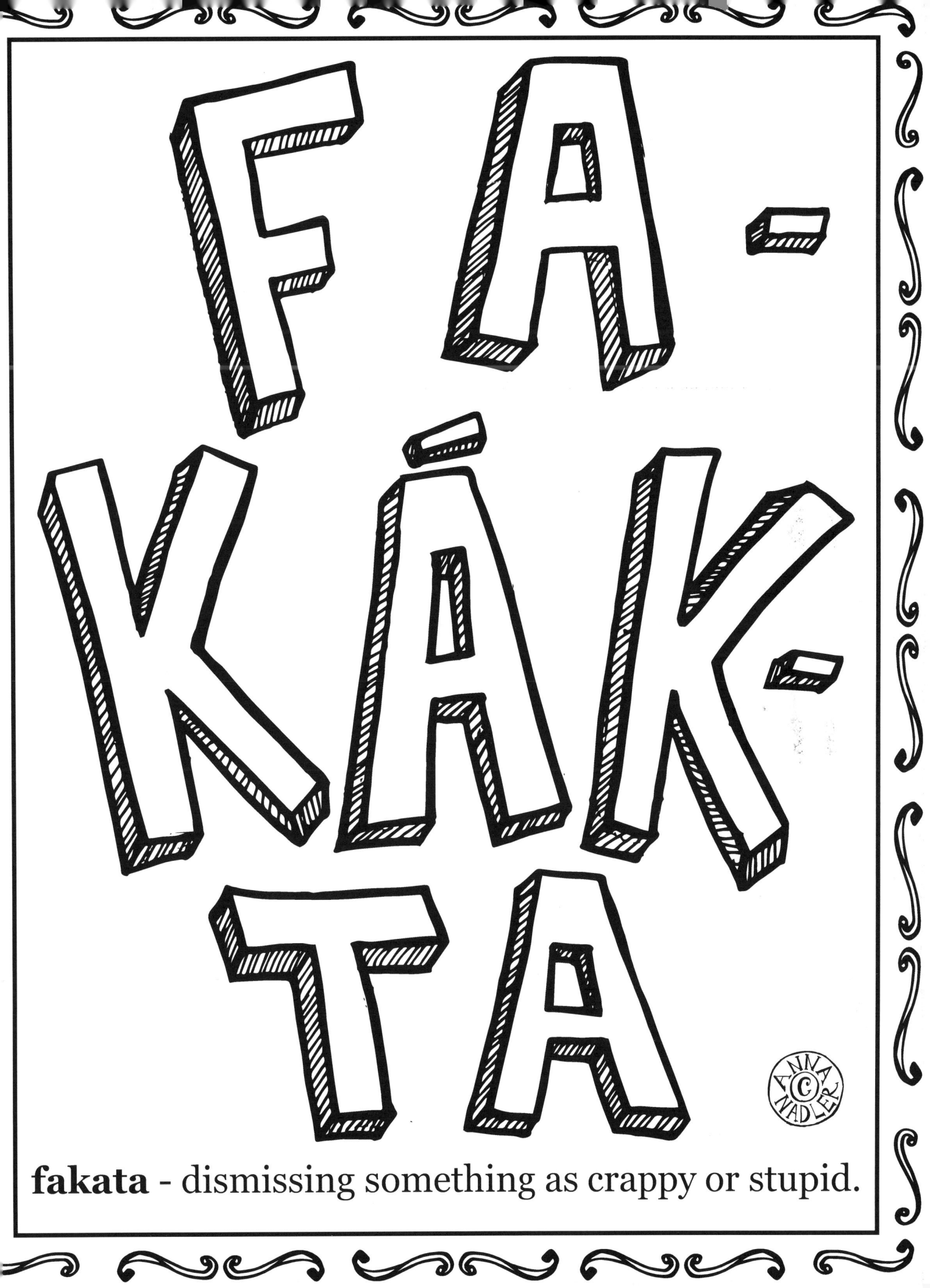

fakata - dismissing something as crappy or stupid.

CHUT-ZPAH

chutzpah - audacity, gull, courage, ardor.
Depending on the use can have a negative air.

oy vey - an expression of exasperation.

© Anna Nadler 2019
© Anna Nadler 2019
© Anna Nadler 2019
© Anna Nadler 2019
© Anna Nadler 2019
© Anna Nadler 2019
© Anna Nadler 2019

SHMUTZ

schmutz - a soiling substance;
"The baby had some schmutz on his face."

SCHMUCK

schmuck - simply a fool, idiot; a stupid person.

tuchus - bottom, rear end.
"She had a nice round tuchus."

© Anna Nadler 2019
© Anna Nadler 2019
© Anna Nadler 2019
© Anna Nadler 2019
© Anna Nadler 2019
© Anna Nadler 2019
© Anna Nadler 2019

Shikker

shikker - an alcoholic or drunkard.

© Anna Nadler 2019
© Anna Nadler 2019
© Anna Nadler 2019
© Anna Nadler 2019
© Anna Nadler 2019
© Anna Nadler 2019
© Anna Nadler 2019

SCHLEP

schlep - to carry a lot of things or a tiring walk.

© Anna Nadler 2019

© Anna Nadler 2019

© Anna Nadler 2019

© Anna Nadler 2019

© Anna Nadler 2019

© Anna Nadler 2019

© Anna Nadler 2019

shlemiel - a slovenly incompetent person.

© Anna Nadler 2019
© Anna Nadler 2019
© Anna Nadler 2019
© Anna Nadler 2019
© Anna Nadler 2019
© Anna Nadler 2019
© Anna Nadler 2019

mench - a true gentleman, an honorable person with integrity.

PUTZ

putz - a big jerk of a person

© Anna Nadler 2019
© Anna Nadler 2019
© Anna Nadler 2019
© Anna Nadler 2019
© Anna Nadler 2019
© Anna Nadler 2019
© Anna Nadler 2019

"-this is the best TV, it's 4D, oled, flat screen, 100 inches, with a harmonic 5K pixel 3D sound."

shpiel - a long sales pitch to convince a customer to buy a thing.

© Anna Nadler 2019
© Anna Nadler 2019
© Anna Nadler 2019
© Anna Nadler 2019
© Anna Nadler 2019
© Anna Nadler 2019
© Anna Nadler 2019

TCHOTCHKE

tchochke - a useless figurine or a trinket.
"My bubbie has many tchochkes in her home."

Shmooze

shmooze - to mingle, to make charming small talk.

© Anna Nadler 2019
© Anna Nadler 2019
© Anna Nadler 2019
© Anna Nadler 2019
© Anna Nadler 2019
© Anna Nadler 2019
© Anna Nadler 2019

mitzvah - a good and selfless deed that can benefit someone or something, a charitable action.

About the Artist

Anna Nadler is an illustrator, graphic designer and author, who lives and works in New York City. She loves drawing fashion, people, animals and architecture, as well as creating unique logo designs for various companies from around the world. You can view more of her work on her website - www.annanadler.com and on social media platforms. You can also find many of her original art books in her Amazon.com book store, where she is always adding new journals, diaries, notebooks, children's books, gift books, planners and coloring books. In her free time Anna loves traveling, singing jazz songs and spending quality time with her friends and family.

Thank you for coloring this book!
If you enjoyed it, please leave a review
on Amazon.com!

Made in the USA
Middletown, DE
16 December 2021